How to Escape the 9-to-5 by Selling Online

A Beginner's Blueprint for Quitting Your Job and Launching an Ecommerce Business From Home

The Fix-It Guy

Copyright © The Fix-It Guy

Table of Contents

Introduction

Hey there, aspiring business mavericks and dream chasers! If you're feeling the soul-sucking monotony of the 9-to-5 grind, envisioning a life beyond the confines of the traditional office cubicle, then buckle up for a ride that might just change your life. This isn't just another "quit your job" spiel; it's an invitation to embark on a thrilling adventure toward financial freedom and professional satisfaction.

Ever caught daydreaming about saying goodbye to the rush hour traffic, the suffocating office politics, and the soul-crushing routines? Well, my friend, you're not alone. In "How to Escape the 9-to-5 by Selling Online," we're not just promising an exit strategy; we're handing you a personalized blueprint for crafting your own narrative, one where you call the shots.

Picture this: Your commute consists of a stroll to your home office, fueled by the excitement of building something uniquely yours. This book isn't about wishful thinking; it's about actionable steps, practical advice, and proven strategies. Whether you're a seasoned professional yearning for a change or a complete newcomer to the world of e-commerce, consider this your backstage pass to a life less ordinary.

We're not selling a pipe dream here; we're selling you the tools, knowledge, and inspiration to turn your passion into profit. From identifying your niche to navigating the intricacies of online marketing and scaling your business to new heights, we've got you covered.

So, if you're ready to ditch the mundane and embrace the extraordinary, if you're eager to transform that side hustle into your main hustle, then turn the page, and let's kickstart the journey toward your version of success. Your dream business is just a click away, let's make it happen together!

Chapter 1

Assessing Your Readiness

Evaluating Your Skill Set

Alright, my future e-commerce rockstars, welcome to the first pit stop on our journey to entrepreneurial freedom! In this chapter, we're diving headfirst into the exhilarating world of self-discovery, where we'll assess your readiness to break free from the shackles of the 9-to-5 grind.

Evaluating Your Skill Set

Step 1: Take Inventory
You wouldn't head into a cooking competition without knowing your way around a kitchen, right? Similarly, before venturing into e-commerce, take stock of your skills. What are you good at? What makes you excited? Jot it down. Don't worry; we're not judging; we're celebrating your awesomeness!

Troubleshooting Tip: Feeling lost? Call up a friend or two for a mini-brainstorming session. Sometimes, others see our talents more clearly than we do.

Step 2: Identify Transferable Skills
Now, let's play the "connect the dots" game. Identify how your current skills can transfer into the e-commerce arena. Are you a pro at communication? Boom! That's a customer service asset. Love playing with graphics? Hello, product imagery! It's like a puzzle, and you're assembling the pieces of your future success.

Troubleshooting Tip: Stuck in skill limbo? Consider a low-risk side hustle or a short online course to beef up your expertise.

Step 3: Embrace the Learning Curve
Newsflash: nobody starts as an expert. Don't let the fear of the unknown hold you back. Embrace the learning curve like a rollercoaster ride—scary at first, but a thrill once you get the hang of it. Whether it's social media marketing or inventory management, Google is your new BFF.

Troubleshooting Tip: Feeling overwhelmed? Break it down into bite-sized chunks. Tackle one skill at a time, and soon you'll be a Swiss Army Knife of e-commerce wizardry.

Remember, it's not about being perfect; it's about being willing to learn and adapt. The e-commerce world is a wild ride, my friend, and you're strapping in for the adventure of a lifetime!

Key Takeaways and Next Steps

1. **Celebrate Your Skills:** Your unique talents are your secret sauce.
2. **Connect the Dots:** Identify how your skills align with the e-commerce landscape.
3. **Embrace the Learning Curve:** It's okay not to know everything; that's what the internet is for!

Now, grab a coffee, pat yourself on the back, and get ready to tackle Chapter 2: Building the Foundation. Your e-commerce empire is just getting started!

Determining Your Passion and Niche

Hey there, passion-seekers and niche navigators! In this chapter, we're diving into the heart of your e-commerce journey, finding your passion and carving out your niche like a digital Michelangelo.

Step 1: Soul-Searching Expedition

What Makes Your Heart Race?
First things first, let's talk about passion. What gets your heart pumping? What could you talk about for hours without getting bored? Whether it's vintage sneakers, eco-friendly gadgets, or handmade candles shaped like mythical creatures, your passion is your compass in this vast e-commerce wilderness.

Troubleshooting Tip: Can't pinpoint your passion? Think back to what you loved doing as a kid. Your inner child might just hold the key to your adult happiness.

Step 2: The Intersection of Passion and Profit
Now, we're not just in this for warm fuzzies (although those are nice too). Let's find where your passion intersects with profit potential. Imagine a Venn diagram with one circle being "What You Love" and the other "What People Buy." The sweet spot in the middle? That's your golden ticket.

Troubleshooting Tip: If you're seeing more passion than profit, don't fret. It might just be a matter of tweaking or reframing. Get creative!

Step 3: Define Your Niche

Narrow Down, Stand Out
In a world where everyone's shouting, "Look at me!" it's time to whisper, "Look at me because I'm unique!" Your niche is your cozy corner of the market. If you love fashion, maybe you're all about sustainable, locally-made accessories for llama lovers. The more specific, the better!

Troubleshooting Tip: Feeling overwhelmed? Think about what bugs you in your current shopping experiences. Chances are, others are annoyed by the same things. Fix it, and voila, you've found your niche!

Key Takeaways and Next Steps

1. **Follow Your Passion:** It's not just a cliché; it's your secret sauce.
2. **Profit in the Sweet Spot:** Find where what you love meets what people want to buy.
3. **Niche Down, Not Out:** Be the llama-loving accessory guru, not just another fashionista.

Understanding the Commitment Involved

Hey fellow trailblazers, in this chapter, we're putting on our serious hats and delving into the nitty-gritty of what it takes to launch your e-commerce business. Spoiler alert: it's not all rainbows and overnight success stories, but hey, that's what makes the journey epic, right?

Step 1: Time Is Your Most Valuable Resource

24 Hours in a Day... Use Them Wisely
Let's be real, building an e-commerce empire isn't a weekend project. It's a marathon, not a sprint. Assess your current schedule, factor in Netflix binges and spontaneous naps, and see where your business fits. Remember, Rome wasn't built in a day, and your e-commerce kingdom won't be either.

Troubleshooting Tip: Feeling overwhelmed by time constraints? Prioritize like a pro. Identify what truly matters and delegate or drop the rest.

Step 2: Financial Commitment

More Than Just a Pretty Website
Sure, you can start an e-commerce business on a budget, but let's talk about the less glamorous side, the financial

commitment. From website hosting to inventory, there are costs involved. Don't panic; we'll navigate these waters together. Think of it as an investment in your dream, not an expense.

Troubleshooting Tip: Budget blues? Start small and scale up. You don't need a Hollywood production budget to kickstart your business.

Step 3: Emotional Rollercoaster Ahead

Strap In for the Ride
Launching your own business is a bit like riding a rollercoaster, you'll experience highs, lows, and the occasional loop-de-loop. Be prepared for the emotional toll. There will be challenges, doubts, and moments when you question your sanity. But guess what? That's normal. Every successful entrepreneur has faced the same.

Troubleshooting Tip: Feeling the emotional whiplash? Build a support system. Whether it's friends, family, or fellow entrepreneurs, having a squad to cheer you on makes the journey smoother.

Key Takeaways and Next Steps

1. Time Is Precious: Be realistic about your time commitments.

2. Financial Planning: Budget for the essentials and view it as an investment.

3. Embrace the Emotional Ride: Entrepreneurship is a rollercoaster, enjoy the thrill and stay strapped in.

Now, grab your commitment cape and get ready to soar into the next Chapter, where we'll be Researching Your Market and setting the stage for your e-commerce triumph!

Chapter Two

Building the Foundation

Setting Up Your Home Office

Hey future e-commerce moguls, welcome to the chapter where we transform your living space into the epicenter of your online business empire! Say goodbye to the 9-to-5 cubicle and hello to the sweet freedom of your own home office.

Step 1: Choose Your Battlefield

Claim Your Territory

First things first, pick a spot that screams "productivity" and whispers "inspiration." It could be a spare room, a cozy nook, or even the corner of your living room (extra points for ninja-level space optimization). Just make it yours, and make it work for you.

Troubleshooting Tip: Feeling cramped? Declutter and organize like your sanity depends on it. A tidy workspace equals a tidy mind.

Step 2: Equip Yourself for Battle

Arm Your Office Arsenal

Now, let's talk about the tools of the trade. You don't need a NASA-level setup, but a reliable computer, a comfortable chair (because your back will thank you later), and a desk with enough space for your genius ideas to flow are essentials. Add in some motivational knick-knacks, and you've got a winning combo.

Troubleshooting Tip: Tight budget? Scour second-hand shops or repurpose what you have. Creativity extends beyond your business, it applies to your office setup too!**

Step 3: Let There Be Light (and Ergonomics)

Shed Some Light on the Situation

Lighting is the unsung hero of productivity. Natural light is the MVP, but if you're in a basement or a night owl, invest in some quality artificial lighting. Oh, and ergonomic furniture? It's not just a buzzword; it's a lifesaver. Your back and neck will thank you later.

Troubleshooting Tip: Eye strain? Adjust your screen brightness, take regular breaks, and blink like you're starring in a slow-motion movie. Seriously, it helps.

Key Takeaways and Next Steps

1. Claim Your Space: Your home office is your sanctuary; make it uniquely yours.

2. Equip Smart: Invest in the essentials, and get creative with your budget.

3. Light and Ergonomics Matter: See the light, and treat your body like the royalty it is.

Acquiring the Necessary Tools and Software

Hey trailblazers, ready to deck out your digital toolkit? In this chapter, we're diving into the exciting world of tools and software that will transform your home office into a command center for your e-commerce conquest. So, put on your tech-savvy cap, and let's gear up!

Step 1: The Essentials

Choose Your Weapon Wisely
First things first, you need a reliable computer and a speedy internet connection. Whether you're Team Mac or Team PC, ensure it's a workhorse that can handle the demands of your burgeoning empire. Your internet? Think cheetah speed, not snail pace.

Troubleshooting Tip: Is slow internet bringing you down? Investigate providers, upgrade your plan, and consider a router reboot. Your empire can't thrive on lag.

Step 2: E-commerce Platform Magic

Pick Your Online Battleground
Choosing the right e-commerce platform is like selecting the perfect battleground. Options like Shopify, WooCommerce, and BigCommerce each have their

strengths. Dive into their features, consider your product range, and find the platform that aligns with your grand vision.

Troubleshooting Tip: Feeling overwhelmed with choices? Test a few platforms with their free trials. It's like dating for your business, find the one that clicks.

Step 3: Payment Gateways and Security Shields

Fortify Your Castle
Protecting your kingdom (and your customers' trust) is paramount. Integrate secure payment gateways like PayPal, Stripe, or Square. These digital knights ensure smooth transactions and shield against the nefarious forces of cyber threats.

Troubleshooting Tip: Customer trust dipping? Display security badges prominently, encrypt your website, and assure them that their data is Fort Knox safe.

Step 4: Design Wizardry

Beautify Your Realm
Your website is your digital storefront, so make it a showstopper. Whether you're a design guru or a rookie, platforms like Canva or Adobe Spark can elevate your

visuals. Don't forget mobile responsiveness; your site should look like a rockstar on any screen.

Troubleshooting Tip: Design-phobia? Opt for clean and simple templates. Less is often more in the design realm.

Key Takeaways and Next Steps

1. Tech Essentials: Ensure your computer and internet are up to the challenge.

2. E-commerce Platform: Choose the one that aligns with your business goals.

3. Payment Fortification: Secure payment gateways are your virtual moat.

4. Design Charm: Make your website a visual masterpiece.

Establishing a Budget for Your Ecommerce Venture

Hey savvy entrepreneurs, welcome to the financial playground where we're turning dreams into dollars! In this chapter, we'll demystify the art of budgeting for your e-commerce venture. So grab your calculators (or open that spreadsheet app), and let's get down to the nitty-gritty.

Step 1: Define Your Battlefield

Map Out Your Financial Terrain
Before you dive into the dollars, map out your business landscape. What are your startup costs? Consider domain registration, website hosting, initial inventory, and any necessary licenses. No need to break the bank; we're aiming for financial wisdom, not financial ruin.

Troubleshooting Tip: Feeling overwhelmed? Prioritize your expenses. Start with the essentials and let your budget evolve with your business.

Step 2: Monthly Operating Costs

Predict the Cash Flow
Now, let's talk about your ongoing expenses. Hosting fees, marketing budget, software subscriptions—these

are your monthly comrades. Anticipate them, plan for them, and make sure your cash flow can handle the ebb and flow of business life.

Troubleshooting Tip: Tight budget? Explore cost-effective alternatives and consider phased investments. Rome wasn't budgeted in a day.

Step 3: Emergency Fund, Your Financial Safety Net

Prepare for Stormy Weather
In the unpredictable world of e-commerce, storms might brew. Whether it's a sudden spike in demand or an unexpected expense, having an emergency fund is your financial safety net. Aim for three to six months' worth of operating expenses tucked away for a rainy day.

Troubleshooting Tip: No emergency fund? Start small and build gradually. Even a little financial cushion can soften unexpected blows.

Step 4: Return on Investment (ROI) Projections

Forecast Your Success
Now, let's talk about the fun part, making money! Project your sales and calculate your expected return on investment. This isn't just number-crunching; it's

envisioning the fruits of your labor. It's the north star guiding your financial ship.

Troubleshooting Tip: Not a financial whiz? Use online calculators, seek advice from mentors, and remember, projections are educated guesses, not crystal ball predictions.

Key Takeaways and Next Steps

1. **Startup Costs:** Map out your initial expenses.
2. **Monthly Expenses:** Anticipate and budget for ongoing costs.
3. **Emergency Fund:** Build a financial safety net for unexpected challenges.
4. **ROI Projections:** Envision your financial success.

Demystifying the art of budgeting for your e-commerce venture.

Chapter 3

Researching Your Market

Identifying Profitable Niches

Greetings, market explorers! In this chapter, we're setting sail on the seas of market research to uncover the hidden treasures, those golden niches that can turn your e-commerce venture from "just another store" into a powerhouse. Get ready to put on your detective hat and let's dive into the world of identifying profitable niches.

Step 1: Follow the Passion Trail

What Makes Your Heart Race?
Remember back in Chapter 1 when we talked about passion? Well, here's where it pays off. Identify your passions and interests, because chances are, there's a tribe out there with similar affections. Whether it's handcrafted leather goods or eco-friendly pet accessories, let your heart guide you.

Troubleshooting Tip: Passionless pit? Ask yourself, "What problem can I solve?" Often, profitable niches hide in solving people's headaches.

Step 2: Spy on the Competition

Know Thy Rivals

No, this isn't a James Bond movie, but we are doing a bit of spying. Check out what your potential competitors are up to. What niches are they dominating, and where are they slacking? Use their successes and failures as a roadmap for your niche discovery journey.

Troubleshooting Tip: Feeling overwhelmed? Pick a few successful competitors and dissect their strategies. It's like a crash course in e-commerce espionage.

Step 3: Analyze Market Trends

Ride the Wave of Popularity

Trends are like waves; catch the right one, and you'll ride it to success. Use tools like Google Trends, social media insights, or industry reports to spot what's hot. Maybe it's sustainable products, or perhaps it's the resurgence of retro items. Keep your finger on the pulse of what's buzzing.

Troubleshooting Tip: Trend confusion? Balance trendy with timeless. You want a niche with lasting power, not just a fleeting fad.

Key Takeaways and Next Steps

1. Follow Your Passion: It's not just about what's profitable; it's about what excites you.

2. Competitive Espionage: Learn from your rivals and spot untapped opportunities.

3. Trend Surfing: Ride the waves of market trends but ensure your niche has staying power.

Analyzing Competitors

Ahoy, business detectives! In this chapter, we're putting on our magnifying glasses and diving into the exciting world of competitor analysis. It's not about copying; it's about learning, adapting, and finding your unique angle in the grand e-commerce stage. Ready to channel your inner Sherlock? Let's go!

Step 1: Identify Your Rivals

Map Out the Competitor Landscape
Who are the players in your field? Identify both the big fish and the smaller contenders. Your goal is not to be intimidated but to understand the lay of the land. Google, social media, and good old-fashioned word of mouth are your trusty allies here.

Troubleshooting Tip: Feeling overwhelmed? Start with a few key competitors. Quality over quantity, my friend.

Step 2: Evaluate Their Strengths and Weaknesses

Sherlock Holmes Mode: Activated
Now, let's play detective. Dive deep into your competitors' websites, social media, and customer reviews. What are they doing exceptionally well? Is it their seamless checkout process, engaging content, or

lightning-fast shipping? Equally important, where are they falling short? Slow customer service, a lack of variety in products? Jot it all down.

Troubleshooting Tip: Information overload? Focus on the key aspects, customer experience, product range, and marketing strategies.

Step 3: Uncover Their Unique Selling Proposition (USP)

The Secret Sauce

Every successful business has a unique flavor, a secret sauce that makes them stand out. What's your competitors' USP? Is it exceptional quality, unbeatable prices, or an unforgettable brand story? Understanding this gives you insights into what customers value in your niche.

Troubleshooting Tip: Struggling to find their USP? Read customer reviews. People often spill the beans on what they love about a brand.

Step 4: Price Point Investigation

The Price is Right... or Is It?

Now, let's talk numbers. How are your competitors pricing their products? Are they on the luxury end, offering premium quality, or are they budget-friendly with frequent discounts? Understanding the pricing landscape helps you position your offerings strategically.

Troubleshooting Tip: Feeling lost on pricing? Factor in your costs, perceived value, and what the market is willing to pay. It's a delicate dance, but you'll find the rhythm.

Key Takeaways and Next Steps

1. Know Your Rivals: Identify both the giants and the hidden gems.
2. Strengths and Weaknesses Analysis: Sherlock your way through their websites and customer reviews.
3. Uncover Their USP: What makes them tick? Find their secret sauce.
4. Price Point Investigation: Understand their pricing strategy.

Conducting Market Research

Hey market mavens, in this chapter, we're strapping on our researcher hats and venturing into the dynamic world of market research. It's not just about collecting data; it's about uncovering insights that will be the backbone of your e-commerce success story. Ready to dive in? Let's roll!

Step 1: Define Your Research Objectives

What Are You Looking For?
Before you start the hunt, know what you're hunting for. Are you seeking customer preferences, competitor strategies, or the latest market trends? Clearly define your objectives to ensure your research is laser-focused.

Troubleshooting Tip: Feeling lost? Start broad and gradually narrow down your objectives. It's like zooming in on Google Maps to find your destination.

Step 2: Embrace Online Surveys and Questionnaires

Poll the People
The internet is a goldmine of opinions, and online surveys are your virtual pickaxe. Tools like SurveyMonkey or Google Forms allow you to create surveys and questionnaires to gather insights directly

from your target audience. Ask about their preferences, pain points, and what makes them tick.

Troubleshooting Tip: Low response rates? Sweeten the deal with incentives like discounts or exclusive content. People love a little extra somethin' somethin'.

Step 3: Dive into Social Media

Social Listening Magic
Social media isn't just for cat memes; it's a treasure trove of real-time customer chatter. Use social listening tools to track mentions of your industry, competitors, and even your brand. What are people buzzing about? What issues are they facing? Your customers are talking; make sure you're listening.

Troubleshooting Tip: Feeling overwhelmed with data? Create filters to focus on specific keywords or topics. It's like decluttering your social media feed.**

Step 4: Explore Industry Reports and Studies

Learn from the Gurus
Industry reports and studies are your crash course in market wisdom. Platforms like Statista, Nielsen, or industry-specific publications often release comprehensive reports. Dive into these to understand

market trends, consumer behaviors, and upcoming forecasts.

Troubleshooting Tip: Overwhelmed by data overload? Focus on the key findings and summaries. You don't need to be a data scientist, just grasp the big picture.

Step 5: Seek Customer Feedback

Your Customers Know Best
Your existing or potential customers are the true north of your business compass. Collect feedback through customer reviews, testimonials, or even direct conversations. What do they love about your competitors? What pain points can you address? They hold the keys to unlocking your market potential.

Troubleshooting Tip: Scared of negative feedback? Embrace it. Criticism is your guide to improvement. Respond graciously and use it to refine your strategy.

Key Takeaways and Next Steps

1. Define Objectives: Know what you're looking for before diving into the research ocean.
2. Online Surveys: Collect insights directly from your target audience.

3. Social Media Listening: Tap into real-time customer chatter on social platforms.

4. Industry Reports: Learn from the gurus in your field.

5. Customer Feedback: Your customers are a goldmine of insights.

Chapter 4

Crafting Your Unique Selling Proposition (USP)

Defining Your Brand Identity

Hey brand architects, welcome to the heart of your e-commerce journey! In this chapter, we're diving into the art of crafting a Unique Selling Proposition (USP) that will make your brand stand out like a beacon in a crowded marketplace. Get ready to define your brand identity and unleash your brand's superpowers!

Step 1: Know Thyself

Uncover Your Brand Essence

Before you can sell yourself, you need to know yourself. What values define your brand? What makes you tick, and why should customers care? Whether it's your commitment to sustainability, your obsession with quality, or your quirky sense of humor, your brand essence is the DNA of your business.

Troubleshooting Tip: Feeling a brand identity crisis? Ask yourself and your team what words or emotions you want people to associate with your brand. It's like creating a vision board for your business.

Step 2: Understand Your Audience

Speak Their Language
Your USP isn't just about you; it's about meeting the needs and desires of your audience. Understand your target customers, what problems are they facing, and how can your brand swoop in like a superhero to save the day? Your USP should resonate with them on a personal level.

Troubleshooting Tip: Not sure what your audience wants? Survey them, engage in social listening, and step into their shoes. Empathy is your secret weapon.

Step 3: Identify Your Unique Value

Stand Out in the Crowd
Here's the million-dollar question: What makes you different from the competition? Whether it's a groundbreaking product feature, a distinctive brand story, or an unbeatable customer experience, identify that unique value proposition that sets you apart.

Troubleshooting Tip: Struggling to pinpoint your uniqueness? Ask your customers directly. They often see aspects of your brand that you might overlook.

Step 4: Craft Your USP Statement

The Elevator Pitch Magic

Condense your brand essence, understanding of your audience, and unique value into a succinct USP statement. Imagine you're in an elevator with a potential customer, your USP should be the compelling pitch that leaves them wanting more. It's your brand's elevator music, and it should be catchy and unforgettable.

Troubleshooting Tip: Is USP sounding bland? Add a sprinkle of personality. Whether it's humor, sincerity, or a touch of quirkiness, let your brand voice shine through.

Key Takeaways and Next Steps

1. **Know Thyself:** Uncover the essence of your brand.
2. **Understand Your Audience:** Speak the language of your target customers.
3. **Identify Your Unique Value:** Stand out in the crowd.
4. **Craft Your USP Statement:** Create a compelling elevator pitch.

Creating a Compelling USP

Greetings brand architects! In this chapter, we're delving deep into the art of creating a Unique Selling Proposition (USP) that's not just compelling but downright irresistible. Buckle up; we're about to sculpt a brand identity that captivates your audience and sets you apart in the bustling marketplace.

Step 1: Unearth Your Unique Angle

The Diamond in the Rough

What makes your brand sparkle? Whether it's a revolutionary product feature, an unparalleled level of customer service, or a commitment to sustainability, unearth the gems that set you apart. Your USP is the diamond in the rough that shines brightest.

Troubleshooting Tip: Feeling like just another pebble on the beach? Dive deep into your brand's essence and extract the uniqueness that others might overlook.

Step 2: Solve a Problem, Fulfill a Need

Be the Hero Your Customers Need

Your USP isn't just about selling a product; it's about solving a problem or fulfilling a need for your customers. Identify the pain points in your target audience's lives, and position your brand as the hero with the solution. Your USP is the cape that makes you their knight in shining armor.

Troubleshooting Tip: Can't pinpoint the pain points? Talk to your customers directly, read reviews, and engage in social listening. Their challenges are your opportunities.

Step 3: Speak Their Language

Become a Fluent Conversationalist
Your USP should speak directly to your audience, and that means speaking their language. Whether it's through witty banter, heartfelt sincerity, or a touch of elegance, tailor your messaging to resonate with your target customers. Your USP is the smooth talker that charms its way into their hearts.

Troubleshooting Tip: Not sure which language to speak? Look at your audience's preferences in communication. Are they all about humor, facts, or heartfelt stories? Adapt accordingly.

Step 4: Inject Personality

Stand Out with Style

Personality is the secret sauce that transforms your USP from mundane to magnetic. Infuse your brand with character, whether it's quirky, professional, or downright rebellious. Your USP should wear its personality like a badge of honor, making it unforgettable in the minds of your audience.

Troubleshooting Tip: Personality crisis? Think about your brand as a person. How would they dress, talk, and interact? Your USP is your brand's fashion statement.

Step 5: Keep it Concise and Clear

The 10-Second Rule
In the fast-paced world of e-commerce, attention spans are short. Craft a USP that can be understood in a blink. Aim for clarity, simplicity, and a dash of intrigue. Your USP is the elevator pitch that captures attention in the time it takes to ride a few floors.

Troubleshooting Tip: Confused about clarity? Test your USP on friends or family. If they don't get it in 10 seconds, it might need some refinement.

Key Takeaways and Next Steps

1. Find Your Unique Sparkle: Unearth what makes your brand shine.

2. Solve a Problem: Position your brand as the solution.

3. Speak Their Language: Tailor your messaging to resonate with your audience.

4. Inject Personality: Infuse your brand with character.

5. Keep it Concise: Aim for clarity and simplicity.

.

Aligning Your USP with Market Demand

Greetings, strategic visionaries! In this chapter, we're navigating the intricate dance between your Unique Selling Proposition (USP) and the ever-shifting currents of market demand. Let's ensure that your brand's magnetic charm aligns seamlessly with what your audience craves. Ready to synchronize your USP with the pulse of the market? Let's dive in!

Step 1: Stay Agile to Market Trends

Surf the Waves of Change

Markets are dynamic, and trends ebb and flow like the tide. Keep a vigilant eye on emerging trends, shifts in consumer behavior, and evolving preferences. Your USP should not be a static entity; it should be agile, ready to pivot and adapt to the changing currents of market demand.

Troubleshooting Tip: Feeling out of sync? Regularly revisit your USP, conduct market research, and be willing to tweak it to align with the latest trends.

Step 2: Listen to Your Audience

The Symphony of Consumer Voices

Your audience is your ultimate guide. Listen attentively to their feedback, engage in social listening, and monitor reviews. What are they saying about your brand and your competitors? Are there unmet needs or desires? Your USP should be in harmony with the desires of your audience, creating a symphony of satisfaction.

Troubleshooting Tip: Missing the beat? Set up feedback loops, conduct surveys, and actively engage with your audience on social media to stay attuned to their evolving preferences.

Step 3: Evaluate Competitor Moves

Spy on the Marketplace

Competitors are not just rivals; they're also valuable sources of market intelligence. Monitor their strategies, observe how they adjust their USPs, and identify gaps or unexplored territories. Your USP should be a strategic move that differentiates your brand while staying aware of the competitive landscape.

Troubleshooting Tip: Feeling blindsided? Regularly conduct competitor analyses, keeping an eye on their USPs and market positioning. Learn from their successes and mistakes.

Step 4: Flexibility is Key

Dance to the Rhythm of Change

Market demand can be unpredictable, and flexibility is your secret weapon. Be prepared to tweak aspects of your USP, whether it's the messaging, product offerings, or customer experience. Your brand should be a dynamic entity capable of fine-tuning its dance moves to stay in rhythm with market demand.

Troubleshooting Tip: Stuck in a rut? Establish a system for regularly assessing and reassessing market dynamics. Embrace change as an opportunity for growth.

Key Takeaways and Next Steps

1. Stay Agile: Adapt your USP to changing market trends.

2. Listen Actively: Your audience's desires should be the melody of your brand.

3. Competitor Awareness: Learn from competitors and identify gaps in the market.

4. Flexibility is Key: Be ready to fine-tune your USP in response to evolving market demands.

Chapter 5

Setting Up Your Ecommerce Platform

Choosing the Right Platform for Your Business

Hey digital pioneers, welcome to the tech-savvy domain where we'll demystify the process of setting up your e-commerce platform. In this chapter, we're navigating the vast sea of options to help you choose the right platform, one that aligns seamlessly with your business goals and sets the stage for your digital success. Let's dive in!

Step 1: Clarify Your Business Needs

Map Out Your Digital Blueprint

Before you start shopping for platforms, take a moment to clarify your business needs. Are you selling physical products, digital goods, or services? Do you need advanced features like subscription options or intricate inventory management? Understanding your requirements sets the compass for your platform quest.

Troubleshooting Tip: Feeling overwhelmed with options? Prioritize your must-haves and nice-to-haves. It's like creating a wishlist for your dream digital storefront.

Step 2: Explore E-commerce Platforms

The Marketplace Showcase

There's no shortage of e-commerce platforms, each with its strengths and quirks. Platforms like Shopify, WooCommerce, BigCommerce, and Magento offer a diverse range of features and scalability. Dive into their realms, explore their interfaces, and envision your business flourishing within their digital landscapes.

Troubleshooting Tip: Confused by the options? Consider your technical comfort level, budget, and scalability needs. Sometimes, the best fit is the one that aligns with your unique business DNA.

Step 3: Assess Ease of Use

Navigate with Ease

Your chosen platform should be your trusty sidekick, not a puzzle to decipher. Assess the user-friendliness of each platform. Are the dashboards intuitive? Can you easily manage products, process orders, and tweak your website's appearance? The smoother the navigation, the more time you can dedicate to growing your business.

Troubleshooting Tip: Feeling lost in the interface? Most platforms offer tutorials and support. Take advantage of these resources to become a navigation maestro.

Step 4: Consider Cost and Scalability

The Budget and Growth Dance
While budget constraints are real, also consider the long game. Your chosen platform should be scalable to accommodate your business growth. Analyze the pricing models, some platforms may start with a lower entry cost but escalate as you scale. Balance your current budget with the potential for future expansion.

Troubleshooting Tip: Budget blues? Some platforms offer free trials. Test the waters and see if the fit feels right for your business before committing.

Step 5: Analyze Integration Capabilities

The App Symphony
Consider the ecosystem around your chosen platform. Can it harmonize with third-party apps and tools? Integration capabilities can streamline your business

operations, from marketing to analytics. Look for a platform that plays well with others and contributes to the efficiency of your digital orchestra.

Troubleshooting Tip: Overwhelmed by integrations? Start with the essentials, like payment gateways and marketing tools. You can always add more instruments to your symphony as your business grows.

Key Takeaways and Next Steps

1. Clarify Business Needs: Define your digital requirements.
2. Explore Platforms: Dive into the realms of popular e-commerce platforms.
3. Assess Ease of Use: Choose a platform that aligns with your navigation style.
4. Consider Cost and Scalability: Balance your budget with future growth.
5. Analyze Integration Capabilities: Ensure the platform can play well with other digital tools.

Designing an User-Friendly Website

Greetings web architects! In this chapter, we're venturing into the realm of web design to craft a digital space that not only captivates but also guides your visitors seamlessly. A user-friendly website is not just about aesthetics; it's about creating an immersive and intuitive experience. Let's dive into the art and science of designing a website that visitors will love to explore.

Step 1: Embrace Intuitive Navigation

The Digital Tour Guide

Imagine your website as a virtual store, and your navigation menu as the signposts. Ensure that visitors can easily find what they're looking for. Keep your navigation simple, clear, and organized. Categories and subcategories should be intuitive, making the user journey smooth and enjoyable.

Troubleshooting Tip: Feeling lost in your site? Test the navigation with friends or family who haven't seen it before. Their feedback can reveal hidden roadblocks.

Step 2: Optimize for Mobile Responsiveness

The Pocket-Friendly Experience

In the age of smartphones, your website needs to be a pocket-friendly companion. Ensure your design is responsive, adapting seamlessly to various screen sizes. A mobile-friendly site isn't just a convenience; it's a necessity for reaching a broad audience.

Troubleshooting Tip: Mobile design blues? Many website builders offer mobile preview options. Fine-tune your design to ensure it looks stellar on the small screen.

Step 3: Prioritize Page Loading Speed

The Need for Speed

Nobody likes waiting, especially in the digital realm. Optimize your website's loading speed to keep visitors engaged. Compress images, leverage browser caching, and minimize unnecessary scripts. A speedy website not only pleases users but also plays well with search engine algorithms.

Troubleshooting Tip: Slow-loading pages? Use online tools to identify bottlenecks and optimize your website's performance. Every second counts.

Step 4: Streamline the Checkout Process

The Seamless Transaction

For e-commerce websites, the checkout process is the grand finale. Simplify it. Minimize the number of steps, ask only for essential information, and provide a progress indicator. The smoother the checkout, the higher the chances of completing the transaction.

Troubleshooting Tip: Cart abandonment issues? Analyze your checkout process for friction points. Eliminate unnecessary steps and distractions.

Step 5: Enhance Visual Appeal

The Aesthetic Symphony

Visual appeal matters. From color schemes to font choices, create a design that aligns with your brand identity and resonates with your target audience. High-quality images, well-designed product pages, and a cohesive visual language contribute to a memorable user experience.

Troubleshooting Tip: Design paralysis? Stick to a consistent color palette, choose readable fonts, and maintain a clean layout. Less is often more in the design realm.

Key Takeaways and Next Steps

1. Embrace Intuitive Navigation: Guide visitors seamlessly through your digital space.

2. Optimize for Mobile Responsiveness: Ensure your website looks great on any device.

3. Prioritize Page Loading Speed: Speed up your website for a delightful user experience.

4. Streamline the Checkout Process: Simplify the journey from cart to completion.

5. Enhance Visual Appeal: Create a visually captivating and cohesive design.

Incorporating Ecommerce Best Practices

Greetings ecommerce maestros! In this chapter, we're delving into the playbook of ecommerce best practices to elevate your digital venture. These practices aren't just guidelines; they're the secret sauce that can turn a good online store into a stellar one. Ready to fine-tune your ecommerce strategy? Let's dive in!

Step 1: Implement Clear Call-to-Actions (CTAs)

The Signposts of Success
Guide your visitors like a gracious host. Implement clear and compelling Call-to-Actions (CTAs) that prompt action. Whether it's "Shop Now," "Subscribe," or "Learn More," your CTAs should be strategically placed and visually distinct, guiding users effortlessly through your digital landscape.

Troubleshooting Tip: Confused about CTA placement? Conduct A/B testing to identify the most effective positions and wording. Your users will show you the way.

Step 2: Leverage High-Quality Product Images

Picture-Perfect Shopping

In the digital realm, your customers can't touch or feel your products. Compensate for this by showcasing high-quality images that offer a virtual touch-and-feel experience. Multiple angles, zoom features, and lifestyle shots can enhance the visual appeal and build trust with your audience.

Troubleshooting Tip: Image overload? Prioritize key product images and consider interactive features like 360-degree views for a dynamic shopping experience.

Step 3: Optimize Product Descriptions

The Art of Persuasion

Your product descriptions are more than just a list of features. Craft them with care, highlighting the benefits and addressing potential concerns. Use persuasive language, weave in storytelling, and make sure your descriptions answer the unspoken question: "Why should I buy this?"

Troubleshooting Tip: Stuck in a descriptive rut? Put yourself in the customer's shoes. What information would you need to make an informed purchase decision?

Step 4: Prioritize Customer Reviews and Testimonials

Social Proof Power

Customers trust other customers. Encourage and prominently display customer reviews and testimonials. Positive feedback builds credibility while addressing negative reviews transparently shows authenticity. Social proof is a powerful force that can sway potential customers in your favor.

Troubleshooting Tip: Scared of negative reviews? Respond with grace, address concerns, and turn negatives into opportunities to showcase your commitment to customer satisfaction.

Step 5: Establish a Seamless Checkout Process

The Frictionless Transaction

Cart abandonment is the nemesis of ecommerce. Ensure your checkout process is smooth and straightforward. Minimize form fields, offer guest checkout options, and provide clear information about shipping costs and delivery times. Every step should bring your customers closer to completing the transaction.

Troubleshooting Tip: Checkout confusion? Test the process yourself and gather feedback. Simplify, clarify, and streamline until your checkout process feels like a breeze.

Key Takeaways and Next Steps

1. Clear Call-to-Actions (CTAs): Guide users with compelling prompts.

2. High-Quality Product Images: Create a visual experience that compensates for the lack of physical touch.

3. Optimized Product Descriptions: Craft persuasive narratives that answer the customer's "Why."

4. Customer Reviews and Testimonials: Leverage social proof to build trust.

5. Seamless Checkout Process: Minimize friction to reduce cart abandonment.

Chapter 6

Sourcing and Managing Inventory

Exploring Different Sourcing Options

Welcome, inventory virtuosos! In this chapter, we're embarking on a crucial expedition into the world of sourcing and managing inventory, an essential element in the symphony of a successful ecommerce venture. From understanding sourcing options to mastering the art of efficient inventory management, let's dive into the details.

Step 1: Understanding Different Sourcing Options

The Inventory Tapestry

Sourcing is the backbone of your inventory, and options abound. Let's explore the key avenues:

a. Manufacturing In-House

If you have the resources and expertise, in-house manufacturing offers control over production processes and quality. However, it demands significant investment and operational oversight.

b. Wholesalers and Distributors
Partnering with wholesalers or distributors allows you to buy products in bulk, often at discounted rates. This option is ideal if you prefer not to handle manufacturing but want control over your product selection.

c. Dropshipping
For a hands-off approach, consider drop shipping. With this model, you partner with a supplier who handles the fulfillment process. You only purchase items when you make a sale, minimizing upfront costs.

d. Private Labeling
Put your brand on existing products through private labeling. This allows for customization without the challenges of in-house manufacturing.

Troubleshooting Tip: Overwhelmed by choices? Consider your budget, expertise, and the level of control you desire. Each option has its pros and cons, so find the fit that aligns with your business goals.

Key Takeaways and Next Steps

1. Manufacturing In-House: Offers control but requires significant investment.

2. **Wholesalers and Distributors:** Bulk buying with control over product selection.

3. **Dropshipping:** Hands-off approach with minimal upfront costs.

4. **Private Labeling:** Customize existing products with your brand.

Implementing Effective Inventory Management

Greetings, inventory maestros! In this chapter, we're diving into the art and science of effective inventory management, a crucial element in the symphony of running a successful ecommerce business. From maintaining optimal stock levels to minimizing costs, let's unravel the strategies that will keep your inventory in harmony with your business goals.

Step 1: Embrace the ABC Analysis

The Inventory Maestro's Score

Classify your products based on their importance. The ABC analysis typically divides items into:

A Category: High-value items that contribute significantly to revenue.
B Category: Moderate-value items with a balanced impact on revenue.
C Category: Low-value items with a minimal contribution to revenue.

Prioritize your attention and resources accordingly. Focus on tighter control for A items, moderate control for B items, and more relaxed control for C items.

Troubleshooting Tip: Feeling overwhelmed by the alphabet? Use sales data to categorize your products. It's like giving each item a backstage pass based on its performance.

Step 2: Set Reorder Points

The Red Alert System

Determine the minimum quantity of each product you should have on hand before placing a reorder. This prevents stockouts and ensures you're replenishing inventory at the optimal time. Consider factors like lead time, sales velocity, and demand fluctuations.

Troubleshooting Tip: Stockouts causing headaches? Adjust your reorder points based on historical sales data and anticipate seasonal trends. Your future self will thank you.

Step 3: Embrace Just-In-Time (JIT) Inventory

The Lean and Mean Approach

JIT inventory involves receiving goods only as they are needed in the production process or to meet customer demand. It minimizes holding costs and reduces the risk of obsolete inventory. However, it requires a robust supply chain and precise demand forecasting.

Troubleshooting Tip: JIT jitters? Ensure reliable suppliers, invest in accurate forecasting tools, and build flexibility into your supply chain to handle unexpected demand spikes.

Step 4: Leverage Technology

The Digital Inventory Maestro
Embrace inventory management software that automates and streamlines your processes. These tools can provide real-time insights into stock levels, track sales trends, and even integrate with your ecommerce platform. Automation reduces the risk of human error and enhances efficiency.

Troubleshooting Tip: Technophobe blues? Start with user-friendly inventory management tools. The learning curve is often shorter than you think.

Key Takeaways and Next Steps

1. **ABC Analysis:** Prioritize your attention based on product importance.
2. **Set Reorder Points:** Anticipate and prevent stockouts with minimum quantity triggers.
3. **Just-In-Time (JIT) Inventory:** Minimize holding costs with a lean approach.

4. Leverage Technology: Embrace inventory management software for efficiency.

Dealing with Suppliers and Fulfillment

Hello, supply chain navigators! In this chapter, we're setting sail into the seas of supplier relationships and fulfillment strategies, an integral part of orchestrating a successful ecommerce venture. From forging strong partnerships with suppliers to ensuring seamless order fulfillment, let's uncover the key strategies that will keep your supply chain shipshape.

Step 1: Cultivate Strong Supplier Relationships

The Supplier Symphony
Building strong relationships with your suppliers is more than a transaction, it's a partnership. Here's how to conduct the supplier orchestra:

a. Open Communication:

Foster transparent communication. Discuss expectations, product specifications, and timelines openly. The more your suppliers understand your needs, the smoother the collaboration.

b. Negotiation Skills:
Negotiation isn't just about getting the best price; it's about creating a win-win situation. Consider factors beyond cost, such as lead times, payment terms, and the flexibility to scale production.

c. Diversify Suppliers:
Don't put all your eggs in one basket. Diversify your supplier base to mitigate risks. Having alternative suppliers provides a safety net in case of unforeseen disruptions.

Troubleshooting Tip: Supplier issues surfacing? Open lines of communication. Discuss challenges and work collaboratively on solutions. A transparent relationship is a resilient one.

Step 2: Optimize Fulfillment Processes

The Fulfillment Ballet
Efficient order fulfillment is the heartbeat of ecommerce. Let's choreograph the fulfillment ballet:

a. Warehouse Organization:
Ensure your warehouse is a well-organized dance floor. Efficiently arrange products, implement clear labeling, and optimize storage to minimize picking and packing times.

b. Automation Tools:
Embrace automation tools to streamline fulfillment processes. Barcode scanners, automated picking systems, and order management software can enhance accuracy and efficiency.

c. Shipping Strategies:
Choose shipping partners wisely. Consider factors like speed, cost, and reliability. Offering multiple shipping options gives customers flexibility and can be a competitive advantage.

Troubleshooting Tip: Fulfillment hiccups? Regularly review and optimize your fulfillment processes. Seek feedback from your team and customers to identify areas for improvement.

Step 3: Implement Quality Control Measures

The Quality Assurance Waltz
Ensure the products leaving your warehouse meet the highest standards. Implement quality control measures:

a. Inspections:
Regularly inspect incoming shipments to catch potential issues early. Address quality concerns with suppliers promptly.

b. Feedback Loops:
Encourage customer feedback on product quality. Act on feedback to continuously improve and maintain high standards.

c. Returns Management:
Develop a streamlined process for handling returns. Understand the reasons for returns and use this information to improve product quality and customer satisfaction.

Troubleshooting Tip: Are quality concerns surfacing? Collaborate with suppliers to address root causes. A proactive approach to quality control prevents recurring issues.

Key Takeaways and Next Steps

1. Cultivate Strong Supplier Relationships:
- Open communication.
- Effective negotiation.
- Diversify suppliers.

2. Optimize Fulfillment Processes:
- Organize the warehouse.
- Embrace automation tools.
- Choose shipping strategies wisely.

3. Implement Quality Control Measures:

- Conduct inspections.
- Establish feedback loops.
- Streamline returns management.

Chapter 7

Implementing a Marketing Strategy

Developing a Comprehensive Marketing Plan

Greetings, marketing trailblazers! In this chapter, we're delving into the dynamic world of marketing to craft a comprehensive plan that will elevate your brand, attract a digital audience, and propel your ecommerce venture to new heights. From building brand awareness to converting leads, let's unfold the layers of a powerful marketing strategy.

Step 1: Define Your Marketing Objectives

The North Star
Begin with a clear understanding of what you aim to achieve. Define specific, measurable, and realistic marketing objectives. Whether it's increasing brand awareness, driving website traffic, or boosting sales, your objectives will serve as the guiding North Star for your marketing endeavors.

Troubleshooting Tip: Objectives feeling elusive? Align them with your overall business goals. Your marketing objectives should be the bridge between your brand vision and tangible results.

Step 2: Know Your Target Audience

The Audience Connection

Your marketing efforts should resonate with your audience. Develop detailed buyer personas to understand the demographics, preferences, and behaviors of your target audience. This knowledge will inform your messaging, channels, and overall marketing approach.

Troubleshooting Tip: Persona puzzle? Conduct surveys, analyze customer data, and engage in social listening to refine your understanding of your audience. They'll guide you on the path to connection.

Step 3: Craft a Compelling Brand Story

The Narrative Symphony

Your brand story is more than a tagline; it's the narrative that connects with your audience on a deeper level. Define your brand's personality, values, and unique selling proposition. Craft a story that resonates emotionally and showcases the essence of your brand.

Troubleshooting Tip: Storytelling struggles? Start with the basics. What inspired the creation of your brand? What problems are you solving? Your story is the heartbeat of your brand.

Step 4: Choose the Right Marketing Channels

The Channel Orchestra
Selecting the right marketing channels is key to reaching your audience effectively. Whether it's social media, email marketing, content marketing, or paid advertising, align your chosen channels with your target audience's preferences and behaviors.

Troubleshooting Tip: Channel overload? Prioritize based on your audience's habits. Where do they spend their time online? Be present where your audience is most receptive.

Step 5: Develop a Content Calendar

The Content Rhythm
Consistency is the heartbeat of successful marketing. Develop a content calendar outlining your planned content across various channels. From blog posts and social media updates to email campaigns, a content calendar ensures a steady flow of engaging material.

Troubleshooting Tip: Calendar chaos? Use tools like editorial calendars or project management platforms to keep your content planning organized and on track.

Key Takeaways and Next Steps

1. **Define Your Marketing Objectives:**
   - Specific, measurable, and realistic goals.
2. **Know Your Target Audience:**
   - Develop detailed buyer personas.
3. **Craft a Compelling Brand Story:**
   - Define your brand's personality and unique selling proposition.
4. **Choose the Right Marketing Channels:**
   - Align with your audience's preferences.
5. **Develop a Content Calendar:**
   - Ensure consistency across channels.

Leveraging Social Media for Promotion

Hello, social butterflies! In this segment, we're diving into the vibrant world of social media and uncovering the strategies to effectively promote your ecommerce business. Social media isn't just a platform; it's a dynamic stage where your brand can shine, engage with audiences, and create a loyal community. Let's unfold the playbook for leveraging social media to its full potential.

Step 1: Choose the Right Platforms

The Social Landscape

Not all social media platforms are created equal. Each has its unique audience and communication style. Consider your target audience and the nature of your products when choosing platforms. Facebook, Instagram, Twitter, LinkedIn, and Pinterest offer diverse opportunities. Select platforms that align with your brand personality and where your audience is most active.

Troubleshooting Tip: Platform paralysis? Start with one or two platforms and expand gradually. Quality engagement trumps the quantity of platforms.

Step 2: Craft Engaging Content

The Content Alchemy
Social media thrives on captivating content. Develop a mix of content types, including:

Visuals: High-quality images, graphics, and videos.
Captions: Craft compelling captions that resonate with your audience.
User-Generated Content: Encourage customers to share their experiences with your products.

Create a content calendar to maintain a consistent posting schedule.

Troubleshooting Tip: Content creativity crunch? Tap into user-generated content, share behind-the-scenes glimpses, or pose questions to spark engagement. The conversation is a two-way street.

Step 3: Build a Community

The Social Cohort
Social media isn't just a billboard; it's a community hub. Actively engage with your audience. Respond to comments, ask questions, and participate in relevant

conversations. Building a sense of community fosters brand loyalty and encourages word-of-mouth promotion.

Troubleshooting Tip: Community concerns? Set clear guidelines for community engagement, moderate discussions, and showcase customer testimonials to build trust.

Step 4: Run Targeted Ads

The Ad Symphony

Social media advertising offers powerful targeting capabilities. Run targeted ads to reach specific demographics, interests, and behaviors. Whether it's Facebook Ads, Instagram Ads, or Twitter Ads, tailor your campaigns to align with your marketing objectives.

Troubleshooting Tip: Ad anxiety? Start with a small budget and test different ad variations. Analyze performance metrics to refine your approach over time.

Step 5: Track and Analyze Metrics

The Analytical Score

Don't operate in the dark, monitor the performance of your social media efforts. Track metrics such as engagement, reach, click-through rates, and conversion rates. Use insights from analytics tools to refine your strategy and focus on what resonates with your audience.

Troubleshooting Tip: Metric mystery? Familiarize yourself with the analytics tools provided by each platform. Regularly review and adapt your strategy based on the data.

Key Takeaways and Next Steps

1. **Choose the Right Platforms:**
   - Align with your target audience and brand personality.
2. **Craft Engaging Content:**
   - Visuals, captions, and user-generated content are key.
3. **Build a Community:**
   - Actively engage, respond, and foster a sense of belonging.
4. **Run Targeted Ads:**
   - Utilize social media advertising for precise targeting.
5. **Track and Analyze Metrics:**
   - Use analytics tools to refine your strategy based on performance.

Utilizing Paid Advertising to Boost Sales

In this chapter, we're diving into the realm of paid advertising, a powerful tool in your ecommerce arsenal. From increasing brand visibility to driving targeted traffic, paid advertising can significantly boost sales when executed strategically. Let's uncover the key strategies to harness the full potential of paid advertising for your ecommerce business.

Step 1: Define Your Advertising Goals

The Ad Expedition

Begin your journey by clearly defining your advertising goals. Whether it's increasing sales, driving website traffic, or promoting a specific product, having well-defined objectives sets the course for your advertising strategy. Each goal will require a tailored approach, so be specific and measurable in your aims.

Troubleshooting Tip: Goal ambiguity? Break down overarching objectives into smaller, actionable targets. This helps in crafting focused and effective ad campaigns.

Step 2: Choose the Right Advertising Platforms

The Platform Selection

Not all advertising platforms are created equal. Choose platforms that align with your target audience and advertising goals. Consider popular options like:

Google Ads: Ideal for reaching users actively searching for products.

Facebook Ads: Offers detailed audience targeting based on demographics and interests.

Instagram Ads: Visual-focused platform, great for showcasing products.

LinkedIn Ads: Effective for B2B marketing and targeting professionals.

Troubleshooting Tip: Platform perplexity? Test multiple platforms initially, then analyze which ones yield the best results for your specific goals and audience.

Step 3: Craft Compelling Ad Creatives

The Creative Canvas

Your ad creatives are the face of your campaign. Whether it's a catchy headline, stunning visuals, or a persuasive call-to-action, craft compelling ad creatives that resonate with your audience. Tailor your creatives to the platform's specifications to ensure optimal visibility and engagement.

Troubleshooting Tip: Creative block? A/B tests different creatives to understand what resonates best with your audience. Continuously refine based on performance data.

Step 4: Implement Targeted Audience Segmentation

The Audience Precision

Precision is the essence of successful paid advertising. Utilize audience segmentation to target specific demographics, behaviors, and interests. Create distinct ad sets for different audience segments, ensuring that your message reaches the right people at the right time.

Troubleshooting Tip: Audience overwhelm? Start with broad targeting and gradually refine based on performance data. Audience insights will guide your segmentation strategy.**

Step 5: Set a Realistic Budget and Monitor ROI

The Budget Balancing Act

Determine a realistic advertising budget based on your goals and expected returns. Monitor the return on investment (ROI) closely to ensure that your advertising efforts are cost-effective. Adjust your budget allocation based on the performance of different campaigns and platforms.

Troubleshooting Tip: Budget blues? Start with a conservative budget, test the waters, and gradually scale up as you identify winning strategies.

Key Takeaways and Next Steps

1. Define Your Advertising Goals:
- Clearly outline specific and measurable objectives.

2. Choose the Right Advertising Platforms:
- Align with your target audience and goals.

3. Craft Compelling Ad Creatives:
- Create visually appealing and persuasive ad content.

4. Implement Targeted Audience Segmentation:
- Precision targeting based on demographics and behaviors.

5. Set a Realistic Budget and Monitor ROI:
- Determine budget based on goals and closely monitor returns.

Chapter 8

Providing Exceptional Customer Service

Building Trust and Credibility

Hello, customer champions! In this chapter, we're embarking on a journey to master the art of exceptional customer service, a cornerstone of any successful ecommerce venture. From building trust to establishing credibility, let's delve into the strategies that will not only satisfy customers but turn them into loyal advocates for your brand.

Step 1: Prioritize Open and Transparent Communication

The Trust Foundation
Building trust starts with transparent communication. Keep your customers informed about order statuses, shipping times, and any potential issues. Provide clear and accessible channels for customers to reach out with questions or concerns. Proactive communication in the face of challenges fosters trust.

Troubleshooting Tip: Communication breakdown? Implement automated order status updates and regularly review customer feedback to identify areas for improvement. Transparency is the key.

Step 2: Offer Personalized Support

The Customer Connection

Treat your customers as individuals, not just transactions. Personalize your support by addressing customers by name, understanding their preferences, and tailoring recommendations to their needs. This personalized touch creates a sense of connection and fosters long-term loyalty.

Troubleshooting Tip: Personalization puzzle? Leverage customer data to understand preferences and purchase history. Implement CRM tools to streamline personalized interactions.

Step 3: Be Proactive in Anticipating Needs

The Proactive Approach

Anticipate customer needs before they even express them. Proactively provide information about upcoming promotions, restocks, or product releases. Address potential concerns before they become issues. Being one step ahead shows customers that you're attentive and committed to their satisfaction.

Troubleshooting Tip: Anticipation anxiety? Use customer feedback, analyze purchase patterns, and stay informed about industry trends to anticipate customer needs accurately.

Step 4: Resolve Issues Promptly and Effectively

The Resolution Symphony

Issues are inevitable, but how you handle them defines your customer service. Resolve problems promptly and effectively. Empower your customer service team to make decisions that prioritize customer satisfaction. A swift and satisfactory resolution can turn a negative experience into a positive one.

Troubleshooting Tip: Resolution roadblocks? Implement a clear escalation process, provide ongoing training for your support team, and learn from each resolved issue to enhance future processes.

Step 5: Collect and Act on Customer Feedback

The Feedback Loop

Your customers hold valuable insights. Actively collect feedback through surveys, reviews, and social media.

Analyze this feedback to identify trends, areas for improvement, and opportunities to enhance the customer experience. Demonstrating that you value customer input builds credibility.

Troubleshooting Tip: Feedback overload? Prioritize feedback based on impact and frequency. Implement changes based on customer suggestions and communicate these improvements transparently.

Key Takeaways and Next Steps

1. Prioritize Open and Transparent Communication:
  - Keep customers informed and provide accessible communication channels.
2. Offer Personalized Support:
  - Treat customers as individuals and personalize interactions.
3. Be Proactive in Anticipating Needs:
  - Anticipate customer needs and provide information proactively.
4. Resolve Issues Promptly and Effectively:
  - Swiftly address and resolve customer issues.
5. Collect and Act on Customer Feedback:
  - Actively seek feedback and use it to enhance the customer experience.

Handling Customer Inquiries and Issues

Hello, customer care virtuosos! In this segment, we're diving into the art of handling customer inquiries and issues with finesse, a skill that can turn challenging situations into opportunities for building trust and loyalty. From the initial inquiry to resolving complex issues, let's explore the strategies that will elevate your customer service to new heights.

Step 1: Embrace a Customer-Centric Mindset

The Customer Symphony

Put the customer at the center of your approach. View every interaction as an opportunity to enhance their experience. Train your team to prioritize empathy and active listening. Understanding the customer's perspective is the first step in providing a solution that truly meets their needs.

Troubleshooting Tip: Customer-centric challenges? Conduct regular training sessions focused on empathy and active listening. Encourage team members to share insights and learnings from customer interactions.

Step 2: Streamline Inquiry Channels

The Accessibility Bridge

Make it easy for customers to reach out with inquiries. Offer multiple channels such as email, live chat, and phone support. Communicate the expected response times for each channel. Streamlining these channels ensures that customers can choose the method that suits them best.

Troubleshooting Tip: Channel confusion? Regularly assess the efficiency of each channel. Use customer feedback to identify preferences and adjust your support channels accordingly.

Step 3: Provide Clear and Comprehensive Information

The Information Beacon

Prevent inquiries by providing clear and comprehensive information upfront. Optimize your website and product pages with detailed FAQs, sizing charts, and product specifications. A well-informed customer is less likely to encounter issues and more likely to make informed decisions.

Troubleshooting Tip: Information overload? Prioritize the most frequently asked questions and make them easily accessible. Regularly update your FAQs based on customer inquiries and feedback.

Step 4: Establish an Efficient Ticketing System

The Resolution Pipeline
Implement an efficient ticketing system to track and manage customer inquiries. Assign tickets to specific team members, set priority levels, and establish clear workflows for resolution. This system streamlines the inquiry resolution process and ensures that no customer concern falls through the cracks.

Troubleshooting Tip: Ticketing tangles? Regularly review and optimize your ticketing system. Ensure that it aligns with your team's capacity and that inquiries are assigned based on expertise.

Step 5: Empower Your Support Team

The Support Champions
Empower your support team to make decisions that prioritize customer satisfaction. Provide ongoing training to enhance product knowledge and customer service skills. Equip them with the authority to resolve issues promptly, fostering a culture of proactive problem-solving.

Troubleshooting Tip: Support stagnation? Regularly assess your team's skill set and identify areas for improvement. Encourage a collaborative atmosphere where team members can share insights and best practices.

Key Takeaways and Next Steps

1. *Embrace a Customer-Centric Mindset:*
  - Prioritize empathy and active listening.
2. Streamline Inquiry Channels:
  - Offer multiple accessible channels with clear response times.
3. Provide Clear and Comprehensive Information:
  - Optimize your website with detailed FAQs and product information.
4. Establish an Efficient Ticketing System:
  - Implement a system for tracking and managing customer inquiries.
5. Empower Your Support Team:
  - Provide ongoing training and empower your team to make customer-centric decisions.

Implementing a Returns and Refunds Policy

Hello customer satisfaction maestros! In this chapter, we're diving into the crucial realm of implementing a returns and refunds policy, an area that, when handled with care, can transform the customer experience and bolster trust in your ecommerce venture. Let's navigate the intricacies of crafting a policy that not only meets regulatory standards but also turns returns into opportunities for customer satisfaction.

Step 1: Craft a Clear and Concise Policy

The Transparency Beacon
Start by crafting a returns and refunds policy that is clear, concise, and easy to understand. Outline the conditions under which returns are accepted, the timeframe for returns, and the process for initiating a return or refund. Use straightforward language to avoid confusion.

Troubleshooting Tip: Policy perplexity? Consider creating an FAQ section dedicated to returns on your website. Use customer-friendly language and anticipate potential questions to make the policy easily digestible.

Step 2: Offer a Fair Returns Window

The Timeframe Symphony

Determine a reasonable returns window that strikes a balance between customer satisfaction and operational efficiency. A fair timeframe allows customers enough time to assess their purchase while ensuring that returned items can be reintegrated into inventory promptly.

Troubleshooting Tip: Returns timeframe trouble? Align your returns window with industry standards and communicate it clearly to customers during the purchase process. Transparency builds trust.

Step 3: Streamline the Returns Process

The Efficiency Pipeline

Create a streamlined returns process to minimize friction for customers. Provide clear instructions on how to initiate a return, whether through an online portal, email, or a dedicated customer service line. Simplify the steps involved and ensure that customers can track the progress of their returns.

Troubleshooting Tip: Returns process puzzle? Test your returns process from the customer's perspective. Identify and eliminate any unnecessary steps that may cause frustration.

Step 4: Consider Offering Prepaid Labels

The Convenience Factor
To enhance customer convenience, consider offering prepaid return shipping labels. This not only simplifies the returns process but also demonstrates a commitment to customer satisfaction. Communicate whether return shipping costs will be deducted from the refund or if returns are entirely free.

Troubleshooting Tip: Label logistics lagging? Negotiate favorable shipping rates with carriers to minimize costs. Communicate the return shipping options clearly to manage customer expectations.

Step 5: Monitor and Analyze Return Trends

The Analytical Lens
Regularly monitor and analyze return trends to identify patterns and potential issues. Track the reasons for returns, customer feedback, and any patterns in returned products. Use this data to refine your product descriptions, address quality concerns, and improve the overall customer experience.

Troubleshooting Tip: Return trend troubles? Implement a system for categorizing return reasons and use this data to inform product improvements. Continuously optimize your offerings based on customer feedback.

Key Takeaways and Next Steps

1. Craft a Clear and Concise Policy:
- Outline conditions, timeframes, and procedures.

2. Offer a Fair Returns Window:
- Determine a reasonable timeframe for returns.

3. Streamline the Returns Process:
- Simplify steps and offer multiple channels for initiating returns.

4. Consider Offering Prepaid Labels:
- Enhance convenience by providing prepaid return shipping labels.

5. Monitor and Analyze Return Trends:
- Regularly assess return data to identify patterns and areas for improvement.

Chapter 9

Scaling Your Business

Strategies for Growth

Greetings, business architects! In this chapter, we're embarking on a thrilling journey to explore strategies for scaling your ecommerce venture. Scaling is not just about expansion; it's about sustainable and strategic growth. From optimizing operations to reaching new markets, let's unravel the key strategies that will set the stage for the next phase of your business journey.

Step 1: Optimize Operational Efficiency

The Efficiency Symphony
Before expanding, ensure your internal operations are finely tuned. Streamline processes, automate repetitive tasks, and identify areas for optimization. Operational efficiency not only reduces costs but also lays a solid foundation for handling increased demand as you scale.

Troubleshooting Tip: Efficiency roadblocks? Conduct regular process audits, seek employee feedback, and invest in technology to automate routine tasks.

Continuously refine your operations for maximum efficiency.

Step 2: Diversify Product Offerings

The Product Portfolio Dance

Expand your product offerings to attract a broader audience and encourage repeat business. Analyze market trends, customer preferences, and competitor offerings to identify opportunities for diversification. Introduce complementary products or variations to enhance your product portfolio.

Troubleshooting Tip: Product expansion puzzle? Conduct market research to identify gaps or trends in your industry. Introduce new products gradually and gauge customer response before further expansion.

Step 3: Explore New Sales Channels

The Channel Exploration

Don't limit yourself to a single sales channel. Explore new avenues to reach a wider audience. Consider expanding to additional online platforms, partnering with retailers, or even establishing a physical presence. Diversifying your sales channels mitigates risk and opens doors to new customer segments.

Troubleshooting Tip: Channel confusion? Assess the preferences of your target audience. If your customers are active on specific platforms, prioritize those for expansion. Experiment and evaluate the success of each channel.

Step 4: Invest in Marketing and Advertising

The Visibility Boost

As you scale, increase your investment in marketing and advertising. Craft targeted campaigns to reach new audiences and re-engage existing customers. Utilize a mix of digital marketing, social media advertising, and other channels to amplify your brand's visibility.

Troubleshooting Tip: Marketing mayhem? Set clear goals for your marketing campaigns and regularly analyze their performance. Adjust your strategies based on the data to maximize your return on investment.

Step 5: Enhance Customer Retention Strategies

The Loyalty Waltz

Retaining existing customers is as crucial as acquiring new ones. Implement customer retention strategies such as loyalty programs, personalized offers, and excellent post-purchase support. A loyal customer base not only boosts revenue but also serves as a foundation for sustainable growth.

Troubleshooting Tip: Retention riddles? Analyze customer data to understand preferences and behaviors. Actively seek feedback and use it to tailor your retention strategies.

Key Takeaways and Next Steps

1. Optimize Operational Efficiency:
* Streamline processes and invest in technology.

2. Diversify Product Offerings:
* Expand your product range based on market trends.

3. Explore New Sales Channels:
* Consider additional online platforms or physical presence.

4. Invest in Marketing and Advertising:
* Increase marketing efforts to boost brand visibility.

5. Enhance Customer Retention Strategies:
* Implement loyalty programs and personalized offers.

Expanding Your Product Line

Hello product pioneers! In this segment, we're diving into the exhilarating world of expanding your product line, an endeavor that requires a strategic approach and a keen understanding of market dynamics. From identifying new opportunities to managing product diversification, let's uncover the strategies that will elevate your ecommerce business to new heights.

Step 1: Market Research and Trend Analysis

The Exploration Expedition
Before venturing into new products, embark on thorough market research. Analyze industry trends, customer preferences, and competitor offerings. Identify gaps in the market or emerging trends that align with your brand. Understanding the landscape sets the stage for strategic product expansion.

Troubleshooting Tip: Research roadblocks? Leverage tools like surveys, social media listening, and competitor analysis to gather valuable insights. Stay attuned to customer feedback and market shifts.

Step 2: Identify Complementary Products

The Synergy Symphony
Consider introducing products that complement your existing offerings. Identify items that naturally pair with your current product line. This not only enhances the shopping experience for customers but also encourages cross-selling and upselling opportunities.

Troubleshooting Tip: Complement confusion? Assess your existing customer base and their needs. Identify products that align with the lifestyle or use cases of your current offerings.

Step 3: Test New Products Gradually

The Iteration Ballet
Rather than launching an entire product line at once, test the waters with a gradual approach. Introduce a few new products initially and closely monitor customer response. Analyze sales data, collect feedback, and refine your strategy based on the performance of these initial offerings.

Troubleshooting Tip: Launch anxiety? Use limited-time promotions or exclusive launches to gauge customer interest. Adjust your inventory and marketing strategies based on the initial response.

Step 4: Collaborate with Suppliers and Manufacturers

The Partnership Waltz

Forge strong partnerships with suppliers and manufacturers to facilitate the expansion of your product line. Communicate your requirements clearly, negotiate favorable terms, and ensure a seamless integration of new products into your inventory. A collaborative approach enhances efficiency and supports growth.

Troubleshooting Tip: Partnership pitfalls? Regularly communicate with suppliers, share forecasts, and maintain transparency to prevent supply chain disruptions. Build long-term relationships for mutual success.

Outsourcing and Delegating Tasks

Hello efficiency enthusiasts! In this segment, we're unraveling the art of outsourcing and delegating tasks, an essential skill for scaling your ecommerce business without overwhelming yourself. From freeing up your time to tapping into specialized expertise, let's explore the strategies that will help you navigate the delicate balance of responsibilities.

Step 1: Identify Tasks for Outsourcing

The Delegation Blueprint

Start by identifying tasks that can be effectively outsourced. Focus on activities that are time-consuming, repetitive, or require specialized skills that are not your core strengths. Common tasks for outsourcing include customer support, graphic design, content creation, and logistical operations.

Troubleshooting Tip: Delegation dilemma? Begin with small, non-critical tasks to build trust with outsourcing partners. Gradually increase the complexity of tasks as you gain confidence in the relationship.

Step 2: Research and Select Reliable Partners

The Partner Selection

Choose outsourcing partners with care. Research potential collaborators, assess their expertise, and check references. Look for reliability, clear communication, and a track record of successful collaborations. Establishing strong partnerships is key to the success of outsourcing initiatives.

Troubleshooting Tip: Partner pitfalls? Clearly define expectations, set performance metrics, and maintain open communication channels. Regularly evaluate the performance of outsourcing partners to ensure alignment with your business goals.

Step 3: Leverage Freelancers and Remote Workers

The Flexibility Advantage

Tap into the pool of freelancers and remote workers to access specialized skills on a project basis. Platforms like Upwork, Fiverr, and Freelancer offer a vast network of talent. Leverage freelancers for tasks such as graphic design, content creation, and digital marketing.

Troubleshooting Tip: Freelancer friction? Clearly communicate project requirements, deadlines, and expectations. Provide thorough briefs and maintain open communication throughout the project.

Step 4: Implement Effective Project Management

The Coordination Dance

Effective project management is crucial when outsourcing tasks. Utilize project management tools to streamline communication, set deadlines, and track progress. Whether using platforms like Trello, Asana, or Slack, ensure that tasks are organized, and collaboration flows seamlessly.

Troubleshooting Tip: Project management predicaments? Invest time in onboarding outsourcing partners and providing detailed guidelines. Establish regular check-ins and feedback sessions to address any issues promptly.

Chapter 10

Overcoming Challenges and Staying Motivated

Common Challenges in Ecommerce

Greetings, resilient entrepreneurs! In this pivotal chapter, we're delving into the art of overcoming challenges and staying motivated, a journey essential for the longevity and success of your ecommerce venture. Let's navigate through the common challenges faced in the dynamic world of ecommerce and uncover strategies to maintain your entrepreneurial spirit.

Step 1: Acknowledge and Embrace Challenges

The Challenge Confrontation
Facing challenges is an inherent part of the entrepreneurial journey. Acknowledge and embrace them as opportunities for growth rather than insurmountable obstacles. Understanding that challenges are a natural component of business allows you to approach them with a proactive mindset.

Troubleshooting Tip: Challenge avoidance? Regularly assess your business operations, identify potential pain points, and develop contingency plans. A proactive stance prepares you for the unexpected.

Step 2: Addressing Customer Satisfaction Issues

The Satisfaction Resonance

Customer satisfaction is paramount, and challenges may arise in meeting customer expectations. Address issues promptly, empathize with customers, and implement solutions that prioritize their satisfaction. A positive customer experience not only resolves immediate challenges but also fosters long-term loyalty.

Troubleshooting Tip: Satisfaction stumbles? Implement robust customer support, actively seek feedback, and continuously refine your products and services based on customer input. The customer-centric approach is your compass.

Step 3: Navigating Supply Chain Disruptions

The Supply Chain Symphony

Disruptions in the supply chain can pose significant challenges. Develop resilient supply chain strategies, diversify suppliers, and maintain transparent communication with partners. This ensures a more agile response to unexpected disruptions, such as delays or shortages.

Troubleshooting Tip: Supply chain snags? Regularly assess the robustness of your supply chain. Establish contingency plans and stay informed about industry trends and potential challenges.

Step 4: Adapting to Market Trends and Competition

The Adaptation Waltz

Evolving market trends and competition require continuous adaptation. Stay agile by regularly analyzing market dynamics, monitoring competitor strategies, and innovating your products or services. Adaptation is not just a response to challenges but a proactive stance to stay ahead.

Troubleshooting Tip: Adaptation anxiety? Foster a culture of innovation within your team. Encourage brainstorming sessions, seek external inspiration, and stay attuned to emerging trends in your industry.

Step 5: Maintaining Work-Life Balance

The Balance Tightrope

Entrepreneurship often blurs the lines between work and personal life. Strive for a healthy work-life balance to prevent burnout and maintain motivation. Set clear boundaries, prioritize self-care, and allocate time for personal pursuits. A balanced life contributes to sustained creativity and resilience.

Troubleshooting Tip: Balance blunders? Schedule regular breaks, establish dedicated work hours, and communicate boundaries with your team. A balanced entrepreneur is a more effective and motivated entrepreneur.

Staying Motivated: The Entrepreneurial Fuel

Amid challenges, staying motivated is the fuel that propels your journey. Here are key strategies:

Set Achievable Goals: Break down larger objectives into manageable milestones. Celebrate small victories along the way.

Find Inspiration: Seek inspiration from success stories, industry leaders, and your own achievements. Surround yourself with a supportive network.

Revisit Your Why: Reflect on the reasons you started your ecommerce venture. Reconnect with your passion and the impact you aim to make.

Continuous Learning: Stay curious and invest in your knowledge. Attend industry events, read relevant literature, and foster a mindset of continuous learning.

Celebrate Progress: Acknowledge and celebrate progress, no matter how small. Positive reinforcement fuels motivation and sustains momentum.

Developing Resilience and Persistence

Hello tenacious trailblazers! In this chapter, we're immersing ourselves in the realms of developing resilience and persistence, a dynamic duo that propels you through the inevitable challenges of entrepreneurship. Let's explore strategies to fortify your spirit, navigate setbacks, and emerge stronger on your ecommerce journey.

Step 1: Embrace a Growth Mindset

The Mindset Metamorphosis
Cultivate a growth mindset that views challenges as opportunities for learning and improvement. Embrace setbacks as stepping stones toward success. A resilient mindset positions you to adapt, persevere, and thrive amidst adversity.

Troubleshooting Tip: Fixed mindset fixation? Challenge negative thoughts and reframe them as opportunities for growth. Surround yourself with a supportive network that encourages a positive and adaptive mindset.

Step 2: Learn from Setbacks and Iterate

The Iteration Evolution

Each setback is a valuable lesson. Instead of dwelling on failures, extract insights, and apply them to refine your approach. Iterate continuously based on lessons learned, turning setbacks into stepping stones toward success.

Troubleshooting Tip: Iteration inertia? Establish a post-mortem process for each setback. Analyze what went wrong, why it happened, and how you can prevent similar issues in the future. Iteration is a perpetual process.

Step 3: Cultivate Adaptability

The Adaptation Ballet

In the dynamic landscape of ecommerce, adaptability is a superpower. Cultivate the ability to pivot when necessary, whether it's in response to market trends, customer feedback, or unexpected challenges. An adaptable entrepreneur remains nimble in the face of change.

Troubleshooting Tip: Adaptation apprehension? Foster a culture of innovation within your team. Encourage open communication and be receptive to new ideas. Embrace change as an integral part of progress.

Step 4: Build a Supportive Network

The Network Nexus

Surround yourself with a supportive network of mentors, fellow entrepreneurs, and friends. Lean on this network for guidance, encouragement, and shared experiences. A strong support system acts as a safety net during challenging times.

Troubleshooting Tip: Support system slump? Actively engage with your network by attending industry events, participating in networking groups, and seeking mentorship. Reciprocity strengthens the fabric of your support network.

Celebrating Milestones and Successes

Hello achievers! In this segment, we're diving into the art of celebrating milestones and successes, a practice that not only acknowledges your progress but also fuels your motivation for the journey ahead. Let's explore how to cultivate a culture of celebration and savor the victories, big and small.

Step 1: Define and Acknowledge Milestones
The Milestone Mapping
Define clear milestones that mark significant achievements in your ecommerce journey. Whether it's reaching a sales target, launching a new product, or expanding your customer base, these milestones serve as checkpoints on your path to success.

Troubleshooting Tip: Milestone ambiguity? Clearly define milestones and communicate them to your team. Align milestones with your broader business goals for a cohesive growth strategy.

Step 2: Create a Celebration Ritual
The Celebration Ceremony
Establish a celebration ritual for each milestone. This could be a team gathering, a virtual toast, or a simple acknowledgment of achievements. Cultivate a positive

and festive atmosphere that energizes your team and reinforces a culture of accomplishment.

Troubleshooting Tip: Celebration neglect? Schedule milestone celebrations in advance. Make them a non-negotiable part of your business culture. Small celebrations foster a continuous sense of achievement.

Step 3: Share Success Stories
The Success Spotlight

Share success stories within your team and with your audience. Highlight the journey, challenges overcome, and the collective efforts that led to success. Inspiring success stories not only motivate your team but also resonate with customers and partners.

Troubleshooting Tip: Storytelling stagnation? Regularly collect and document success stories. Use various channels, such as social media, newsletters, or blog posts, to share these narratives. Authenticity amplifies impact.

Troubleshooting Tip: Gratitude scarcity? Integrate expressions of gratitude into team meetings, emails, and day-to-day interactions. A culture of appreciation elevates morale and team cohesion.

Conclusion

As we conclude this transformative journey through the pages of "How to Escape the 9-to-5 by Selling Online: A Beginner's Blueprint for Quitting Your Job and Launching an Ecommerce Business From Home," take a moment to reflect on the incredible odyssey we've embarked upon together.

In the chapters preceding, we've traversed the terrain of ideation, resilience, and strategic implementation. From assessing your readiness and crafting a compelling Unique Selling Proposition (USP) to expanding your product line and navigating the challenges of ecommerce, each chapter has been a compass guiding you through the multifaceted landscape of online business.

This book isn't just a blueprint; it's a companion, a guide that has walked beside you as you've faced challenges head-on, celebrated victories, and honed the skills needed to thrive in the ever-evolving world of ecommerce. Whether you're in the early stages of launching your business or a seasoned entrepreneur seeking new strategies, I hope this journey has provided the insights, motivation, and practical tools needed for success.

Remember, entrepreneurship is not a destination; it's a continuous voyage of growth, adaptation, and innovation. The digital realm is dynamic, and your ability to evolve will be your greatest asset. As you move forward, stay committed to your vision, embrace challenges as opportunities, and savor the sweetness of every success, both big and small.

In the grand tapestry of ecommerce, you are the master weaver, crafting a narrative that unfolds with each product launched, each customer served, and each milestone surpassed. Your story is unique, and your journey is a testament to the spirit of resilience and persistence that defines the heart of every entrepreneur.

May your ecommerce venture continue to flourish, evolve, and leave an indelible mark on the digital landscape. Your odyssey has just begun, and I am confident that the chapters yet to be written hold boundless possibilities.

Here's to your success, innovation, and the unwavering spirit of the ecommerce entrepreneur!

Wishing you fulfillment and prosperity on your ongoing adventure,